Remains to Be Seen

David Rushmer

Remains to Be Seen

Shearsman Books

First published in the United Kingdom in 2018 by
Shearsman Books
50 Westons Hill Drive
Emersons Green
BRISTOL
BS16 7DF

Shearsman Books Ltd Registered Office
30–31 St. James Place, Mangotsfield, Bristol BS16 9JB
(this address not for correspondence)

www.shearsman.com

ISBN 978-1-84861-582-3

Copyright © David Rushmer, 2018.

The right of David Rushmer to be identified as the author of this work has been asserted by him in accordance with the
Copyrights, Designs and Patents Act of 1988.
All rights reserved.

Acknowledgements
Some of these poems were previously published in the following journals or websites:

Angel Exhaust, Archive of The Now, BlazeVOX, Epizootics, E.ratio, First Offense, Great Works, Horizon Review, Molly Bloom, Moria, Oasis, OxMag, pen:umbra, Shearsman, Spine, This Corner, Tremblestone, Yule Log.

And the following pamphlets:
Sand Writings (Ion Press 23, London) 1991
The Family of Ghosts (Ourhouse, Cambridge) 2005
Blanchot's Ghost (Oystercatcher Press) 2008

And an anthology:
Sea Pie: a Shearsman Anthology of Oystercatcher Poetry,
edited by Peter Hughes *(Shearsman Books),* 2012.

Contents

Remains to Be Seen (1990-2005)

Spoken Bodies	11
Locus Amorphous	14
The Oracle Bone	17
Untitled	19
The Voice of the Desert	20
The Hostage (after Blanchot)	27
Night Snow	28
Centrifugal, Centripetal	29
To Be Dead Language	32
Remains to Be Seen	33
Sound Asleep	34
The Punctuate	35
"…literature is going toward itself…"	36
A Lace of Shadows	37
Where You Spoke	41
The Origin	44
Into the Forgetting	45
"…one can only write…"	46
Panspermia	47
Journey through the Body	49
"…when there is nothing…"	50
Eclipsed	51
Sand Writings	61

Utterly (2008-2010)

Utterly	71
Utterly II	73
Utterly III	74
Utterly IV	75
Utterly V	76
From Tongue to Tongue	77

Blanchot's Ghost (2008)

The Disappeared	81
The Stream	83
The Significant	85
The Passage	86
The Unfolding	87
The Edge of the World	89
Second Version of the Imaginary	91
Of Embrace and Yet Drifting	92
Reflections of the Corpus	93
The Possibility	95
The Duplicity	96
The Solitude	97
The Source	98
The Translation	99

Another Tongue (2009-2014)

Ghosts After Music	103
Hidden by Leaves	105
Written Off	107
A Blooming	109
Lance'd	110
Waiting to Happen	111
Waiting to Happen II – The Experience	115
Waiting to Happen III – The Movement	116
Holding Your Breath	117

No Matter (2014-2016)

No Matter	121
The Drift	122
The Casualties	123
The Radiance	124
Impossible Skin	125
Vibrating Skies	126
No Matter II	127

Shell	128
Surface, Memory	129
I Sing the Blood	130
The Form	131
The Memory in Our Wings	132
The Parallels	134
The Mother	135
Palimpsest	136
The Book in Mind	137
Tears in the Fabric	138
Grave Air	139
The Event Horizon	141
Substance	142
Transmission	143
The Sky You Spoke	144
Oresteia	145
This Body	146
Re/Dis/Member	150
The Wake	154

Remains to Be Seen

Spoken Bodies

Body 1

"…) ossified
petrification of tidal waves
bathing the hands

perfumeries of absence

Body 2

…; haunted

light liquefies, in salivated mists
stained vacancy
of the wound

healed. (closed mouth

Body 3

gape)

meditation.

forged from the fabric of sleep
the waking hand trembles over the assembling body

the shape of,
what is, "otherness"

Body 4

the tongue deciphers amorphosity
and the body is born out
of the body

expelled,   ,into the distance
of equidistant breath

voice,   )exposed
to the hungers of the frost

Body 5

where light forms
the new body is crystallised
and beckoned to venting

the full bloomed rose
shells it heart
to the silence

the hand that stirs the breathing
encloses
surrounding the phallus of sound

erectile tissue
scarred where the wound
becomes female

reopening herself

Body 6

she is a voice
conversant with snow

petrified and blackening
in the light

Locus Amorphous

I

    efflorescent

body
suspended
    in the air

held
in a net
    of blood

the white of the eye

moon blinks into sight
genesis of liquid bone

flow &
counterflow
flood
    of emptiness

clouds web

ghost of rainfall

II

a hole
    right through me
where the wind
    passes its hand
    welcomes the tide
the names of the dead
    on her lips

drowned voices
corpses of foam
    thrown up by the sea

    the gasp for breath
in an ocean of silents

III

a hole
    right through me
where the wind
    passes its tongue

    licks my wounds

    silent dawn

    vocal eyes

IV

to come
    out of nothing

or

    to touch myself
in your reflection

The Oracle Bone

body without form
beneath milk-teeth stars
fist of wind
encircling sound

the cries of birds
leave their imprint
in the bone

—

in the beginning
a pause
foetal comma
coil of thought
the sleeping messenger
awakens in the bulb

forming fingers
prizing open the mouth
feeding the host with sunlight

hands entwine
the current of the blood
solidifies the spine
tongue poking
the belly of the sky

—

my teeth shall fall
from my skull like rain

the dreams of the dead
flow into the ocean

Untitled

unborn tongue
belly-up
in the mouth

musical rain
moon-painted surfaces
rippled hieroglyphs
chatter to the open sky

the wind wraps her hair
around the bone
solidifies the violence
of the flow

and into the silence
sound flowers
the cold blooms
effluviate

meat
nascent
in the dark shell

The Voice of the Desert

first & foremost
"I am desert"

the emptiness
preceding rain

from the masculine
the projection

                becoming female
                on the page

"I copulate"

and there is solitude.

"I scrape,
    gently at the whiteness
        where the wind
          has moved me"

and suddenly, imperceptibly
  "she is here"

(as if the wind…
…opening its mouth)

expanding
expanse

I watch her
she, whom I have made from desire

always moving
away from me

entering the desert
to spawn her

she escapes
through my breathing

_____
_____

it is raining

"she scrapes the mirror
from my face"

The Hostage (after Blanchot)

"…suspended

in this night

at a loss

to the immediate

my breath held

  by another

Night Snow

sky unloaded of its ghosts

Centrifugal, Centripetal

"...Reader's lips ceased to move from the sixteenth century onwards as reading became silent, left the mouth and its articulation, and burst into the space of the mind. This internal reading completely modified our relationship to the text, which no longer triggered a linear impulse, but a spacial relationship..."
                                                    Bernard Noël

words
crashed
back
into
the
skull

a
reading
behind
the
eyes

absorption
from
the
dead
side
of
mirrors
slow
collapse
into
the
space
of
origins

magnetism
of
reversed
polarities

explosion
into
the
white
light
of
silence
/

blush
of
lunar
current

pulse
of
leaf
or
petal

unfolded
flame
of
open
hand

capillary
foliate

feeds
the
flowering

a
bruise
of
ink

embered
glow
of
internal
eyes

To Be Dead Language
(fragments from a translation of 'L'été Langue Morte' by Bernard Noel)

world of wind
     indifferent love
       & beauty's breath
we watch it evaporate

     to darkness behind
the tongues' advent
illuminating
     day's aimlessness

a stone's shadow
     it's pause within
     washes meaning
for doubt is enough

     the collapse of the visible
tongue's gap
and echoes farewell
     petals you

     your name already old
       in spoken air

Remains to Be Seen

before the first word fallen
cry of an animal
imperceptible distance

my life a circle
written in its centre

absence of my breath
carved in your shape

the liquids
through its channels

giving birth to a movement
birds set black flames
alight in the sky

Sound Asleep

sound
    asleep
with your bones
        and the rain that falls
    on the naked wind
outlines the shape
        of when I am dead

the name you gave me
    came from my mouth
in yours
    my hands dissolving
    rubbed out by our blood

inside our body
    a music of disappearing
    beneath your skin
approaching reflection
    urges him towards lightning
        flushing a carcass
        blushed a bruising sky

her mouth
    abandoning my ghost
    in the torn flesh of air
we have come the distance
    the whole of the eyes

The Punctuate

you don't know
you are born

a puddle of ink
where your face used to be

the sky is a graveyard
to plant your fingernails

the wind has eaten
the remains of your body

night is a liquid
in place of your tongue

pouring your face
into the veins of the sky

the moon hangs pregnant
belly full of unborn stars

the blood will rush back into your mouth

as she tears at your face
at the moment of birth

your body shall remain
abandoned in the sky

empty naked
riddled with punctuation

> *"literature is going toward itself, toward its essence, which is disappearance"*
> Maurice Blanchot

where you have been
is my waiting place

when I see you
words come

meat my collision in space
the sky drinking from its liquid mirror

A Lace of Shadows
(for D. H.)

I

    "night

    a lace of shadows

rain

bruising my heart
    with its kisses

that opening

    morning

a blade
shape
    from your tongue

cuts the throat of the horizon

      "unfolds the movement

II

my fingertips
beneath your skin

sleep on your breath
collision of my breath

dawn pours its gold
on our bones

III

      "…indifferent to the possibility

absorbed

daylight
a force

    beyond the hands

   emptiness

               weighs its own gravity

IV

approaching reflection

        "withdraws

            again from nothing, formed

the interior
in terror

inferior

mirror to mirror

      "smash my face in the mirror

Where You Spoke

ghost fed

on the darkness
 of your eyes

         "where you spoke"

made a hole in me

air punctured

breath   in flames

the earth slips

like sand through my fingers

"you speak my body to its shape

The Origin

the origin is transparent
the ghosts in your veins
show through your paper skin
a desert of light
to hide your naked bones
voices pass through you
the sky has eaten your tongue
the wind hangs by its nostrils
from your skull
night stretches your skin
across its face
pokes its tongue
through your lips
holds you open
like a perfume
circulates you
in its blood
& in its breath

Into the Forgetting

into the forgetting
the eyes turn back
in their sockets
reflect their interior
the wind gathers
pushes its tongue
into the mouth
bellows my lungs
into wings
a weightlessness
lifts
suspended
inside the body
as if the body
took flight
inside the body
turning our gaze
into ourselves

> "... one can only write if one arrives at the instant towards which one can only move through the space opened up by the movement of writing ..."
> *The Gaze of Orpheus* —Maurice Blanchot

night.
"

    "opens its wings to us

nocturnal kiss

    "poured the darkness through your veins"

impossibility
the universe
    in your eyes

I take your tongue
    to my grave

    "what space between us"

the instant
    of flame

held in your hand
you look at me
the earth disappears

a movement of birds
contains us

where the night
speaks our skin

Panspermia

a mother's tongue
coiled in the stomach

language collapses
in the elemental body

                dormant panoply
               of tight sewn lips

                               lightning illuminates
                                      scar tissue

                               tongues of birds
                               burn in the wind

   your reflection
in the swelling juice

of the liquid eyes of raindrops

constellations of saliva
magnetised into the moon's
bag of blood

held in prelacteal
mist

                          tongue splitting
                            aural hymen

                          tide spills itself
                          through the teeth

                                                  sky and earth
                                            horizontal union

                                                        their skins
                                      pierced by the kiss of rain

                                              rippling in the passage
                                                of gravity's sentence

Journey through the Body

moment after the world has been achieved
    when speech advances
in flames

words
bleed through the skin

flushing a carcass

tear my lungs
with the spread of your wings

the sky
  a fist
    inside my veins

> "... when there is nothing, that is where the image finds its condition, but disappears into it..."
> *Two Versions of the Imaginary* —Maurice Blanchot

you fall into
the space of me

body caressed
by a graveyard of sky

filled the air
with your bones

your eyes
a locus of images

mouth drawn open
in the rain

poured myself
through your nakedness

lilac prickle
of my bruised tongue

tattoos of rain
to wash the other away

pulled your flesh
to my lungs

inhaled you
like sunshine

Eclipsed

I

        eclipsed, &
ash-formed

remnant of the sun

but speech is for the hollow
now lost,
where the outline
tore

and thrust the body

    —   out.

feeling, &
beginning not,

    to.

in the emptiness of words

you

me.

we cannot escape the Body

there is always you & "…

…………", &

Condition of the failure.

(hunger fed by hunger…

the body is stretched
to become its vacancy

II

it is only "hands"

conversing from the interior

working to expel
"Itself

will of infinity
to displace me

into the finite,

    "gesture"

voice
centripetalled light

hands
quinquefoliate

beneath
the sun

where the body yearns to light
forms the skin of its movement

unspeakable hymen
of the mouth

white open wings

dispersing

utterance

        "voice
sucked into the infinite

I breathe in your body

your voice expels me

III

  ,& here

the waiting
out-
side

of the page

  ,& you
how fragile

stroked the skulls
  of butterflies

lips of unquenchable waters
saliva frosted

genesis
of bone

slow tearing in the circulation
of immensity

the body will open
only to drown us

you are the part of me
that I cannot steal
by facing the mirror

always you are here
in what I speak

what I do not.

what I set free
in you
is without name

and without name
identity enfolds

absence facing its absentee.

IV

adoration of the earth

    :moon

facing away
always

she

bodily expansion
of absence

I have fed you
from my forgetting

I hallucinate your breath
sleeping

where the mirror
caught you

light
cindered

at last the darkness
feeds me

gesture, or
dilemma

it is shown
through the skin

already torn from
what was

)…& becoming
Not

briefest thought
within a world of white flame

burning the wingtips
of waves

absolution of nothing
eternity

is only the weak point
of memory

the sky and the sea
have mated

lost offspring
of no horizon

Sand Writings

written in sand.

or, perhaps
voices

left for dead

left agape
the will of tearless cries

swallows breath
wordlessly

gorged:——
on emptiness

I cover my mouth.
you never left
a trace

———————

tongue laps
the sand

your voice
stings

the breeze
against my face

word,   or notes
hung in the air

before they burst
into silence

sound

circles

my tongue presses into you.

again,

the day broke

———

your voice closed
inside your mouth

entering you
I am lost

voice leaks
page mists

white spittle

whiteness)
      hardly
      daring

          to mark
          you

only sentiment
or the will
for blood

pressing my finger
into the moon

or,

gently taking
your face

for a mask

desire
or its will
for failure

the sound of you
rushing
into me

walking
into the space
you had left

"surrounded"

the sky rolled over
naked belly

revealing thunder

the rainbow ends

cutting myself
the air
sucks me dry

words returned
through clefts
in the sky

where lightning scarred

tongue in my mouth

———

leapt into forgetfulness
its fullness,

        empties.

utter silence,
or to utter it

, language
speaks me

this habit
or ritual

———

offerings
left for the tide

voice stiffens
word mucal

ossified

or,

carrying me
within the bone

space closing
air-tight

or a place

where even my breath
will turn on me

like a word

I once said
held against you

penumbra tightening
its reach

constricting the circling
of the centrifuge

words choke

or rush
to meet waves

Utterly

Utterly

      all that was   will be.Ours
    in the spine of the voice
             collapsing
as we approach sound

    between immensity
and eternity
    evolved wonder

        "float like a mote of dust
     in the morning sky."

     the hands of unseen ghosts
     carry us to worlds that
        never were

                 We
       that dimensions and distance

            is a place.

        vantage
    waves of space,
       to the edge of
          dust

light without centre

Utterly II

night of possibility
sky torn from your hands
    & thrown to earth

an empty lung

    collision of gravities
secret breathing
behind the mirror
bleach white skeleton of a bird

Beyond is another. Unspoken/Unflown
    approaching disappearance

the air around me
gives up its gravity

    plume of fire

    .

    streaming by us

    widowed wind

moonlight under my fingernails

between bone and laughter
a hysterie of language
    in the body's organs

"The blood and the image that was in the blood"

Utterly III

Emerge in another part of
space,

the blink of an eye

material and memory
tear down the sky

lightning's ghost
a kiss
in torn sheets

Ours. Will be   "all.

      the possibility

      the sunshine

an impact on the
    eye:

a sense of waiting
between collisions

Utterly IV

this point

    a double
       on the one hand

        luminosity
          of another law

'we can no longer go our separate ways'

Utterly V

torn
from their gaze

blue wings of the sky
wrapped around my eyes

From Tongue to Tongue

voyage
>> to the centre of language
> for what is nominated
> and what
>> nominal

>> naming,
>>> the articulation
> of the plurality
> and the finality
>> of things

>> gives birth
> and takes life
> in the same breath

>>> "but the tongue is still born

> my tongue
>> reeks
of the dead
>>>> and my rotting speech
>>> falls apart in the air

> thrown into the shadow
>> that grows to become the earth
>>> hurtling towards me

Blanchot's Ghost

"...this grave which was exactly his size, his shape, his thickness, was like his own corpse, and every time he tried to bury himself in it, he was like a ridiculous dead person trying to bury his body in his body..."

from *Thomas the Obscure* – Maurice Blanchot

The Disappeared

        what you did not write has been written
            absorbed   indifferent to
                the possibility
                      to language, behind
nothingness,
it seeks
                to be found
      redirection, the displacement
             beyond this: null,
   this emptiness inside,   open up
     reflection, with its own gravity
   withdraws
again from nothing
      formed,
   this presence
   :as an interior
              twilight,
           unfold it
  inscribe it in space,
  in his eyes
      the movement which carries him forward,
        Or that opening

   morning

        the impossibility
        exists and merges

the source of his existence
        when it was inside merges
     the outside
       night of possibility
        what bursts

enclosed in the sentence "
>> disappeared, it has become
> a reflection of them.
colliding
> is disappearing.
>> secret intimacy
>>> Another
>>> living substance
>>> to merge with him.
someone else's voice,
>>>> pure night
>>> itself within
>> cannot be grasped.

> outside of him,
> absorbed into the workings
> a nothingness
>> in the act
>> of disappearing.

The Stream

                      the stream
                essence dissolved
                    its disappearance
                    delights it.
     pure nothing
silence
for him alone.
        himself, in his heart
    the operation   carried out
   denies the substance
attach itself   outside itself.
turning towards the world:
                pure intimacy
   whatever it neglects   whatever it abandons,
indifference   passion.
    torn apart
                    one another.
      pure absence
               immobilizes him
perpetually absent,
   shifting also forms   his presence,
     each stage of himself   demands everything
      "Obliterate
       speak in you".
      deepness of the night
      and he is the origin,
     does nothing but come
       the surface of the world;
    condemn and to love
transforms the world,
   unreal before then
only a desire, I can turn it over
        something which was not there
         which was there before

                              the transformation
                            condition of the world
turn change me,
        in another form, touched,

The Significant

       to withdraw
in his own image
     the immobility
   its resemblance surrendered

The Passage

                unable to remain
        I become other.
            remains in the margins
            crushing.
                limitless: we
everything he is,   everything he is not.

                                possesses the infinite:
                                limit escapes him.
        substituting for the world
                it is that distance,
            makes this distance
                the capacity to grasp
                        to go to sleep.
    it vanishes, to justify itself
the universe,
      everything at once,
      divided into irreconcilable moments
      urging him towards
                nothingness.
embodied in literature: the passage
                elsewhere
there is nothing
  everything has been
      an intimacy to himself.
          death, so to speak:
it is in the disappearance
When the blade falls

The Unfolding

                                    swallowing a mouthful
                                      of water."
                                            empty
point
        no longer any interior. It is the moment
                          it is his truth.
                  clinging

            body of work,
      a passion, a passion
                  driven to blood,
                          within this circle
I bring her close, she is everything

        unfold: speech
it is inside
the open
    the absence
in this light
floods
        speaking
        he annihilated death
    into which they had disappeared;
    enclosed in daylight,
my language;
    detached herself,
                    death at every moment
              between us as the distance
            my absence from being
        "trembled in the depths;
                  I do not speak
                      nothing speaks,
              as if it were

                        nothing but its absence,
eternal
                        the one hand,
            infinite movement
            infinite absence
                        nullifying what encloses it
            formless and nameless
         nothingness within the limits
         language, in motion
               wavered between each word,
                              repose of noon,
            search for this moment
                        in this pebble
                        in the tomb
                  into the daylight,
            darkness of this flower,
                        language, abandoning
                  inscribed in the world
                        after the world has disappeared,
               obsession of the night;
      impossibility of dying.
                        as passive as the corpse enclosed
                              it is the movement
            abolished:
            the darkness of
                        the day,
            of its beginning,
               which merges
                  when it has not yet appeared.
               grasp the movement
                              to exhaust it
      aimless passion,   violence, with everything
                  to come into the world.
                        form, a force
         transparency of the earth:
            flutter of
      closing wings

The Edge of the World

to shatter the world:
    the annihilation
        a horizon
            enters
            another,
  now there is nothing
      towards the advent of the world;
          at the edge of the world
            a moment within
              grasp
      where the world can be seen
    slipping
  impregnated
                      neither being nor nothingness
          completely eliminated
the edge of nothingness;
      opens a path for itself
          to each of its moments
              indefinite movement
there to be forgotten
      it is transparent
          the forces of the world
              absolute nature
                  and also indifference
        pivoting invisibility
        entering the daylight
        deep within itself
      a point of instability
        changing everything
disintegrating force,
  hidden in the intimacy
  detached
              possibility,
            to one another

laceration, the source
disappearance of every way out
    deep inside every word

Second Version of the Imaginary

    when nothing disappears into it
neutrality
      indifferent depth   nothing is affirmed, it inclines
   the intimacy
        menacing nearness
  next to the infinite
       a reflection. We believe
the absence
an interval
to open another day
         pushed forwards
         pure
        transparent
          unformed
          passivity
  makes us submit
  everything falls back
       awakening
        then we imagine
        that distancing
appearing as something that has disappeared
         again touches
        the reflection
           disembodied

Of Embrace and Yet Drifting

what we call   evades
                   the living person
               in the absolute calm
               the place,
               left to him
               is missing
                     presence established
                         how fragile
the place where one dies
       remains
         in the depths of its presence
support of indifference, the yawning intimacy
                   situated here.

no longer of the world
                    a return
      indeterminate
presence and proximity. This is the impression
               close to the condition
a familiar
distance
    dying
"in your arms"
          "displaced"
     untouchable,
of embrace and yet drifting

Reflections of the Corpus

      when this moment comes,
remains appear
    withdrawn from us, just when
        broken
            passions
    come back towards us
    designates   distance
    draws towards the day
by resemblance
            retained in order
            formal virginity
its own image   no longer this world, in which
            possibility, a shadow
      behind the living form
    reflection
    absorbing
        truth and change
        nothing more. It is the equal
    rare moments
    more distant, close to
        his own ghost
disappearing in its use, this appearance
resemblance and reflection
            "   "

abandoning themselves
there is nothing   surrendered itself to
        everything that appears
            haunting obsession
      one does not escape
               a place (
) we know
      tranquil immobility we have dressed
    as close as possible   by obliterating
    the others who remain

>   assigned to it.
>   any moment   where we are without
>   an invading presence,
>   a certain moment
>   of that error
>   what is endless fall
> to another place
>   unlocatable,
>   full of names,
> affirmations of identity,
>   within the limits drawn
>   everything obliterating
>   making it equal to
> this slow disappearance,
>   by transforming
>   the white substance
>   a moment of ecstasy

The Possibility

for a moment, the possibility
        a horizon,
     a place
where the image of passion
the heart most pure
   does not escape the other

The Duplicity

        the duplicity of the world
          a beginning
          death is sometimes the work
connected to finitude
        the possibility
        dissolves too
          to go beyond it
the other   as horror
           always remains
                  dissociate where distance holds us
                remote movement
                far from ourselves
          intimate passion
          along this transformation
as reflection   from the movement
          outside ecstasy
          enters equivocal limit
          any interval
      absorbed its reflection
          draws itself up
      to the universe
      to create itself
      to act on the impossible
a movement to recapture negation
constantly threatening to vanish

The Solitude

    solitude.

          the search for indifference
          sustaining
          of the day.

    thrust to one side,
dismissed
          destroys in another

        the infinite still sees
        enclosed space
        in the form
        of the missing
        pursues the incomplete

          the infinity

the infinity and the movement of everything
the scattered world diverted from the whole

        it is.

    nothing more. Outside of that,
belongs to the solitude of the world
language protects language by disappearing
        framework of absence
        never to hold the remains
        belongs to the risk.

The Source

    If we want their source.
the violence of a beginning
      occurs the innermost part
never grasping its approach
        this void
            ties him to his absence
            never knows to reverse the dead.

The Translation

with the subtlest
music   the flourish
of words,

    gesturing in the text.   "The Experience
        a sentence

     to stretch between
     white blossoms
        & fault lines,

  after all forms of

        path
        disappearing

  snowfall
to bury my tongue

Another Tongue

Ghosts After Music

      surrounded by
    her movements
   her twisted body boneless
        eyelids beat
burning
iris
     the lathe of wings
          the silent
darkness of sleep
   again and again
     longing
dusk and dew follows with grace
the fine-boned skull
     and flesh-warmed tongue
     white flash
   a snowflake
pale kindling flushed heart
     dark-blooded mists
        of hanging light
there are ghosts after music
    tomb
    black silence beyond sleep
websoft the opening body
   it slips
   and falls away
to a shimmering breath
          pure
     sunlight
    her hand and silence
   offers torn leaves
of white light
   opening mouths
in the raw spring
    naked

                the voice
            walks the corridor
in a dark coil of hair
                the grave
        of her empty house
        withdrawn
passage on her belly   her suffering eyes
        broken symphony of breath
soft fillet
        the hair of graves
                and polished stones
her body flowers silence
flooded   grey vapour
        voice echoing
                spread my passing
I kissed the other
                against himself
                    fallen beyond cold stars
        coils of sucking lips
veins burn
            a flame sliding space

Hidden by Leaves

the last line
      spoke of this life
"floating   a dream that vanishes
   lift their eyes
      carry them to
         all directions
   on a journey
   he grasps at
   the air
      there is an attempt
      that which remains unsaid
            words are
landscape
   image
      stand out against the snow
  accidental, of the beautiful
    disappears in mirrors
  to further place and time
     so often attains
       the eternal
     and the movement
         of our feelings
  and elsewhere in the world
to write
   the only
     root   If we
examine
forms
   of those who remain
to reflect
       changes
     the location of the grave
     with almost pleasurable expectation
     to move

      to the next world
        these preparations
        toward
    the dying, allowing
        sometimes
            a collection
                the essence of all things
empties
to the world beyond
    death or the house of its relatives
    merges into
    contact
                  who calls the dead
                  in midsummer
    to their place of birth
        it is said
  effigies, or
      bodies of water
          a force superior
        for his most private thoughts
        hidden by leaves
the boundaries of this world.

Written Off

following sentence
            beneath furnished experience
     writing the destruction of voice

    every point   neutral

   oblique space slips away identity
   the body writing doubt
        no longer acting outside itself

    voice origin   enters death

consciousness centred on his passions
as if the end transparent
      point language to the place

leading activity
     to pure himself
     fragment of the movement being
disappointment entrusting the hand
     the principle experience itself

    an empty process to be filled
    an emptiness outside to exhaust it
an act of writing utterly
    transforms the absent

     divided lives work simultaneously
in no way a being   there is no other
     time eternally an operation of rare form
     no other act is uttered

II

        I sing having buried the pathetic hand
              passion and necessity
the hand cut off
        a field releasing a space

tissue drawn
from the centres of eternal gesture
        never to rest himself
the interior to translate the dead
the passion draws tissue
        of deferred multiplicity

the thread and the space not pierced
evaporates a system of literature
        liberates its source
nature woven   this perpetual duplicity

drawn from   and entering into one place

focused hitherto the space inscribed
holds together a trace it sets aside
writing the birth of death.

A Blooming

these shores
    are language tide
chewer of corpses
his errors
    the portals of discovery
from reflection
    from what shall be
all quiet from where we lay
    this is the flower
        in question

beautiful light
shadows reaching up walls
    dead breaths
transmigration of the soul
guiltless as the unsun snow
    to be a mother
    filling the belly
minor chord
falling space silky scrapey
you will drink me piping hot
    the pity of it
    all must go through it
    in silence
goodbye to my sleep
all shape poured out of bed
our first death
    veil of tears
        blooming.

Lance'd

The words,
    to think
        we enter
memory and devotion
from there.
from which I come
        unfamiliar
            flesh
    details
distance
    a landscape
        reading
                . There,
        took shape
                the sound of
,   this
    nearness.

    everything,
        through
            silence,
        movement,
fill the chamber with blood
opened
into language,
    and in search of it.

Waiting to Happen

        threatened
    an other
reaching
      close up, impossible
                      infinite
                              the edge of
            without being
          yet to come
         every arrival
       comes upon
         withdrawn space
            detached from night   sleepless
     the circle
reforms   a centre
       of unity,
  Writing
      separated from the star.
           disorientation
          a fall
           unlimited
        and simple loss
       purity of destruction,
    if all things
     returned to absence   if nothing were
          renders death
             for withdrawal
  abandoning ourselves
    we would escape it.
   The disaster, depriving
death,
the tragic dissolving
          all internal movement,
       to entertain this

                        edge
                to forgetfulness
                    outside
                            the condition
suffering
goes under   utterly passive,
drawn from all sight
                    carries us,
                            untouched,
                    face to face

            we forget, endlessly.
                        forgetfulness
                does not come
                        ,one dies
                    it invites escaping
                    as return
                    absolute;
                It comes   , and yet
                        would come to us from beyond.
                        to write,
                                    outside passion
        of forgetfulness.
    It will speak in you
            of silence
            passed beyond danger,
                the mark
                    under threat
                                an unspoken thought.
    I do not know how I arrived
        without knowing
            the advent
                outside being
drifting away
flight of thought
limitless space
        delivered of stars,

                    whoever dreamed
                would liberate us
            at the twilight
            disrupts and overflows every silent affirmation
            the singularity
                does not disrupt solitude,
immobile forgetfulness
                        in the passivity of
                    all words   ,as if
        the burn   ,the annihilation
            like someone who would no longer enter
        penetrated
        remembrance
of gentlest difference, and this difference
        only as impure loss.
            the disaster is thought
        of the outside
            already touched a silent effect
there is not explosion except what escapes the very possibility,

                    the limit of writing.
it is dark
        the movement of anonymity
        in the present.
writing is
surrendered to a boneyard
            I fulfill myself
        in the anonymous continuity
        between the encounter with death
point where we abruptly dissolve
        the chance of being
            without body
        before words separated from meaning, broken
                this desire to lighten of tears
        lets himself go
                speech that flows and flows away
                        broken reserve, a deep

                    capacity
in advance of a sign
at a distance to words.

The Experience (Waiting to Happen II)

impossible death
the experience to escape
    this collision
within itself

      except by forgetting. I will speak

   which has not yet begun

   in the dreams
   at our birth
      language not to remain
         a desire, one must destroy
         one constant blow
           of speech

The Movement (Waiting to Happen III)

                              movement
to the limit. Still, it is possible
    as we write
        approaching the limit
     perilous threshold
       of being turned back.

Holding Your Breath *(for Wang Bang)*

1

hands
        kiss the earth

        listen

the sentence echoed

watching petals

        this world split
        motionless
              weeping

2

folding you
   yellow
blossoming homeward

time sinks into the sand

your body
   the indentation
   of a body

a whole year
listens to its rumour

loves becoming
driven
   towards

3

no dream
    together
walked the edge
of each other's arms
where I long

4

every finger
                tips
  stars

      my footsteps
        to drink

No Matter

No Matter

we have taken to the air.

        to occupy it, in ways
only in dream).

this process
    to merge with it

discoveries of black,
    inhabiting,
    entered with
        forms
          imagining.

no matter

      the other centred the bone

    metal and water,
    singular in form

    between two words
    accidents, and appearances
of the disturbance
        motion and flows,

an object, a body

        to isolate it from itself
                open up a space
      in other words
    appeared.

The Drift

        drift into thinking
    at intervals only

Souvenirs translated as nightmares

           when he speaks
    of what he has not yet discovered

    verbal coincidence
       or vapour,

    being diffused into the body,
    between the outer and the inner world.

View of the sun: the same obscurity.

The Casualties

We thrive by casualties.

        the unity of sensations,
    this way of thinking,
        locates   not just in space,
but also in the body
  of fluids inherited
  or suggested
spilled out of the narrow spaces

        the two waves
  effluvium,
          from living beings.
    voluntary, concentrated and manipulated.
    The curious blend

the idea   between the matter
        and the forces to which they were subject.

  the conductor of the vibrations

     diffused form of matter,
                as of the breath, after
it has served its purpose.

        Visible substances
flesh, bone, blood
      vibrate into us,
will act and perform it.

The Radiance

        diffused radiance.
my *book of skin*.

        spills out from the body

forms a second skin,
    obedient to
    itself

    a shining mist
    the scattering of light
        invisible forms.

kind of richness,
    There is another

    tradition of hostility
airborne

    where the radiant
    broke out from objects

        where it flows

Impossible Skin

    experience of the limit
his identity
    from this point on
        vulgar error of   defense

      now writing   his own name,

  absorbed in the tissue
  pelted his imagination.

        "to slowly wend its way
an umbilical between worlds"

        "with both ends burning"

  A physical
      telling and retelling
  markings and deformities

      concludes by reprinting
    his target.

    The argument
  maternal
  movements
      develop a mind over
            the skin

      the feeling of closeness
  determines the forms taken

Vibrating Skies

    skies vibrating
engaging the disturbance
           launching
      the middle air

    simply changing colour fields
        inside the cloud
             birthing new forms

the vessels are nothing

      the confines of gravity,
private visual space,
    sunlight and wind,
     actuality and dream,

  keep moving
to almost certain destruction

No Matter II

    the skin grows by volume

        the formation
            a paradigm

        the projection
            of its development

        coats the blood

    It

will be drawn – like a shell of possibilities

    over the mind

Shell

tongue of flame
    where thirst was born

        the suck of light
        that of the universe

            white skin. Words bled
            to expand forever.

    more matter
        followed by a contraction,

            evoking another skin
    edges curled
        light coming from the centre.

            A cloak of invisibility, to suggest
the absence

whiteness is an ideal

    a bodily mask
of receding space

    projecting being

        what shines through the eyes
            shall contain it

Surface, Memory

                a surface   memory)
          coming to mark.

           rather be the flame,
                              escaping
  its resemblance, with itself.

    The primary touch

spark/
  or inscription.
leaves no trace,
                            a ripple:
  below the surface
      an invisible layer
         silent groove

     before language, the foundation

          between self and other,
a contact between layers: 'This utterance

     wanting the skin
       to see
       through the mouth

     tongue lain
       to waste

I Sing the Blood

                I sing the blood,

             skinned,
             and carried
    on vocal cords

    the vital spirit
    in principle

    object of exhaustion,

drawn from the current
    moonflight
    in the veins

           until the advent

      where the image sang

The Form

the form it took inside the body

                                    slowing,
                this way of thinking

                        becoming
      pure flow,
   as an absolute ideal,
matter
of thought.

                       this subtle fluid
           to penetrate all bodies
                 at a distance,

the substance
       of mirrors
    intensified by sound,

    universally
diffused,

               It is a force
               of a body

                    in memory only

The Memory in Our Wings

     as if the possibility
were birthing its own ghost

the ether
        to give up
        all material bodies

    human documents,
          beams of spinal light
             relinquish them
                against the corpuscular theory

        it goes, without saying.

    in the form of waves
       & the brutal loss
to injury.

We carry the memory in our wings.

II

    wound, spread,
       where
       the tongue formed
the branching vessels of language
    attached to the mother,

son followed
earth.

the paper bodies

    bloody containers of matter
       open, burning

       night recovered
         his voice
in lightning veins
asunder.

We carry the memory in our wings.

The Parallels

      wings of sunlight

      inhaled
      in the breath

open
the image of each other

      mirrors passing through me.

      time
      without pattern,   movement
      or history

the sense alone
is activity.

"light scraped from beneath the fingernails

          to offer something
              from a cloudless sky.

The Mother

reading *your mother*
        in a poem

                      a book of water

                      another
                      current threaded

                      full moon blossomed

            morning

            laced through with
                  blood
                  dust
                  the colours of butterflies

      like ribbons of air
memories *evaporating*

Palimpsest

    opening,
                    this haunted body
method of the book

    spore blooming, tongue blossomed
words source   their surface
                       as the skin is scraped

       archeological.

   spaces and depths
            in language
                she finds

              reading a composition
      on the skull

    structure is
         material

                the silences
              engraved

The Book in Mind

    originally,
        the whole book
in one's mind.

another
    blank

    alone in the woods
with the strangers

    embedded,

            in silent dialogue
            with those who are gone,
            and those yet to come

    Set them both aflame

we can assimilate,
two heat sources
    into
        one blossom of
            smoke

Tears in the Fabric

                before our eyes

nothingness and infinity,
      a radical emptiness

           the ignition,
           subtle matter spoken

           the backbone of light
           and its slow collapse

               the harmony of movements
   fills the lungs with gravity

  collisions on the wing

           releasing dusts
           on the skin

           the fragments
composing random scores

      sings the pattern
           in the blood

      a mask of hands
           opening and closing
        night and day
      of the book

      gathering feathers of laughter
      and the dead
between their sheets

Grave Air

      many forms, encountered
    without material form,

the air   informed
              the absent

    open fields
        stretch the limit of the horizon

            "*the echoes net the blood*

    between death and air
    the beginning,

    arresting place for the body
engraved

    unburied birds
and thirsty dust

        "*traces the inside of the mouth*

      within this moment,

vocal trajectory, mapping an arc
    made empty
        in my offerings. The embers
           dripping
              in clouds of smoke
      & burnt plume.

    The pattern blaze

            far beyond

      scores the space
     injecting
music in the eye.

     air burial
ashes scattered

     in flight or mute ability.

The Event Horizon

        A sudden flowering
            to speak

The spoke
    event,   occurring, breathless,

        to float in the vessels
           of consciousness and drift
      the system
    of disturbance
becomes
    the first
        presence
           in the sphere of bodies
    expanding in all directions
        to exhale those places

    a passage provided by the air
    infinitude of the sky

another form in aural space

    torn from the fire
    in spoken dance
        & displacement

Substance

in a beginning of substance,
    who speaks of it
        ancient
            state of grace,
    or matter

    fire or dust
in the birthing sky
        which could pass
           in the same time's breath
aerial, or liquid form

            "we are already dissolved
        in the voice

      these gestures
disappear in their own musics,
or
the silence beneath the wing

    words cast across oceans
  the wind set sail
long before us

    In the search for essence
        they drink their own reflections

Transmission

leave earth behind

the transmission
        is drowned in
        another
            dream
            broadcast
            from eternity

                "*all the colours fade*

        I am suckled
      by the air
      each breath ceded
                to internal code

                the beyond
on the other hand
                blurring
    form to the edges

an oscillation
        vibration in the inner ear
        of the wind

      but the tongue should go further

           finality, the burn,
of material substance

     cut open by the eyes

The Sky You Spoke

    the sky
       is returning
                my tongue

the stars burn
    empty space

       the mind
              roof
                   rotted
a bodiless humming

           the birds
      fell burning
  in bright flames
    that eat my heart

its white core
bursting
    the winds'
fluttering robe

sailed

    vocal light

the word dreams
    you spoke

Oresteia

I

the flame
    awakes

II

murmuration

my heart
    born in a cloud of birds

III

      the first rains
unleashed
   their spears

This Body

    the possibility of the corpus
sentenced

opens a door to its wounds

      describing its progress

        between the action
in the muscle

    the blind delivery
of
blood, flowing into every outcrop
        as the particles

      drawing together

                      move a bodily frame

                      force, that also drives

            an annihilation of space

                    only your eyes place me

II

the body associates
   of light

      tear the moment again

         voice splintered

            the slow penetration
            of matter

breath felled
   on a cracked mirror

III

        The opening
            daylight
                of thorns & shadow

enlightened
    the lips of the horizon
        opined

IV

    become the image
             breathed   the whispering of secrets

                        into every space

            the carrying
                        of elements
a visible   field

The day is now beginning
        on your fingertips

Re/Dis/Member

        delight in

the unseen

    the organs
    in the face
    of writers

    that performed
slices

      another focus
in the lightning

II

    the first image is that of the eye

        opening

watching
    holds fast the
        image

    as long as one can bear

III

    reappearance in various forms

This hole

  like time, is meaningless
burnt through

    stones
    in place of the eyes.

IV

       causing the pain in other words,

an impact

       immediacy

              the regard

                 objectifies
              her erotic activity

but she remains
carrying an internal monologue
    as the story
    of her seeing

    she can view it all

    the dead
in which I am floating

The Wake

    the pupil dilates
            from the vigil
          of sleep

The message

        motivated
        by the act
radiating from deep
    pooled blood

                        to fluctuate
              in slumber

        an insect's wings
                skimming the surface

        (before melting

    explain the vanishing
            of memory

codes *of the body*
    that drift and stream

    dimensions of   /winds, vapours,

      and the chambers
of muscular force.

    opening of/   opening

          painted,

    a void

    seen

as the interior space
    of flowers, shells,
    an unblinking eye at the centre,

  ripples

www.ingramcontent.com/pod-product-compliance
Lightning Source LLC
Chambersburg PA
CBHW031149160426
43193CB00008B/302